I0473111

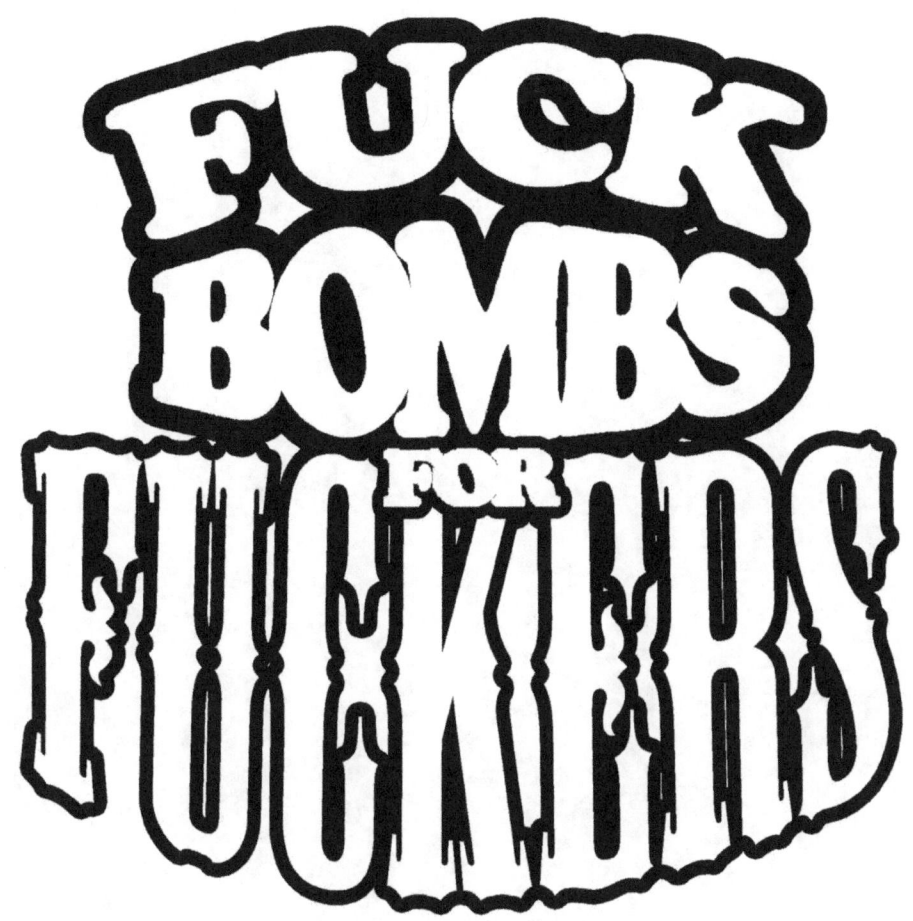

SWEAR WORD COLORING BOOK

Kate Blume
blumesberry art

Page Addie Press

Fuck Bombs For Fuckers is Copyright© Kate Blume of Blumesberry Art 2017 All rights reserved
No paragraph, photograph or part of this publication may be reproduced, stored in or introduced to a retrieval system, or transmitted, in any form (electronic, mechanical, photocopying, recording or otherwise) without the prior permission of the publisher or in accordance with the provisions of the Copyright Designs and Patents Act 1988. This book is sold subject to the condition that it shall not, be lent, re-sold, hired out, or circulated without the publisher's prior consent in any form of binding or cover other than the one in which it is published.

ISBN:978-0-6480768-1-0 paperback.
BIC Subject category: 1. Arts & Photography. 2. Drawing-coloring books for grown-ups
3. Craft, hobbies 4. Self-help-art therapy & relaxation 5. Self-help-anger management

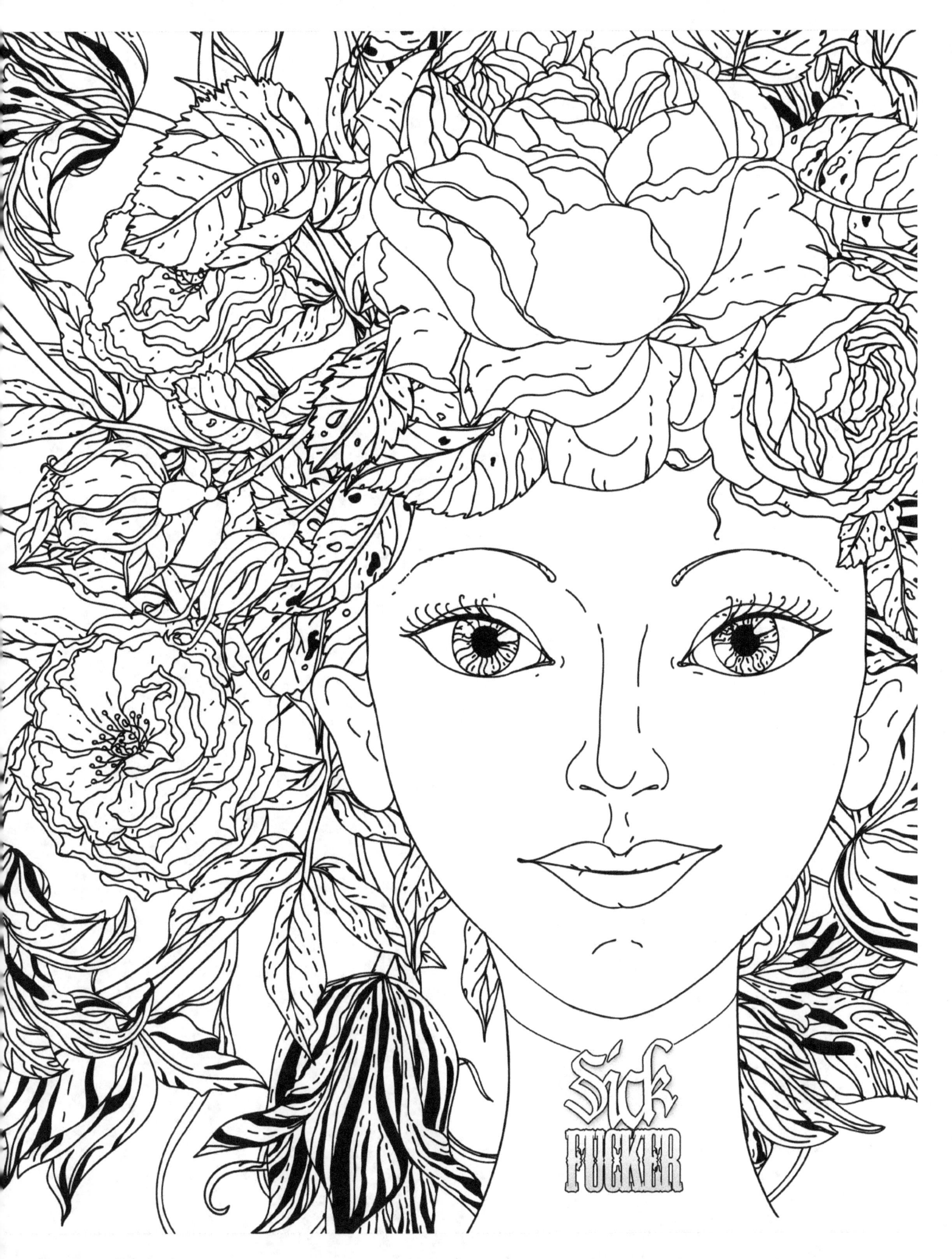

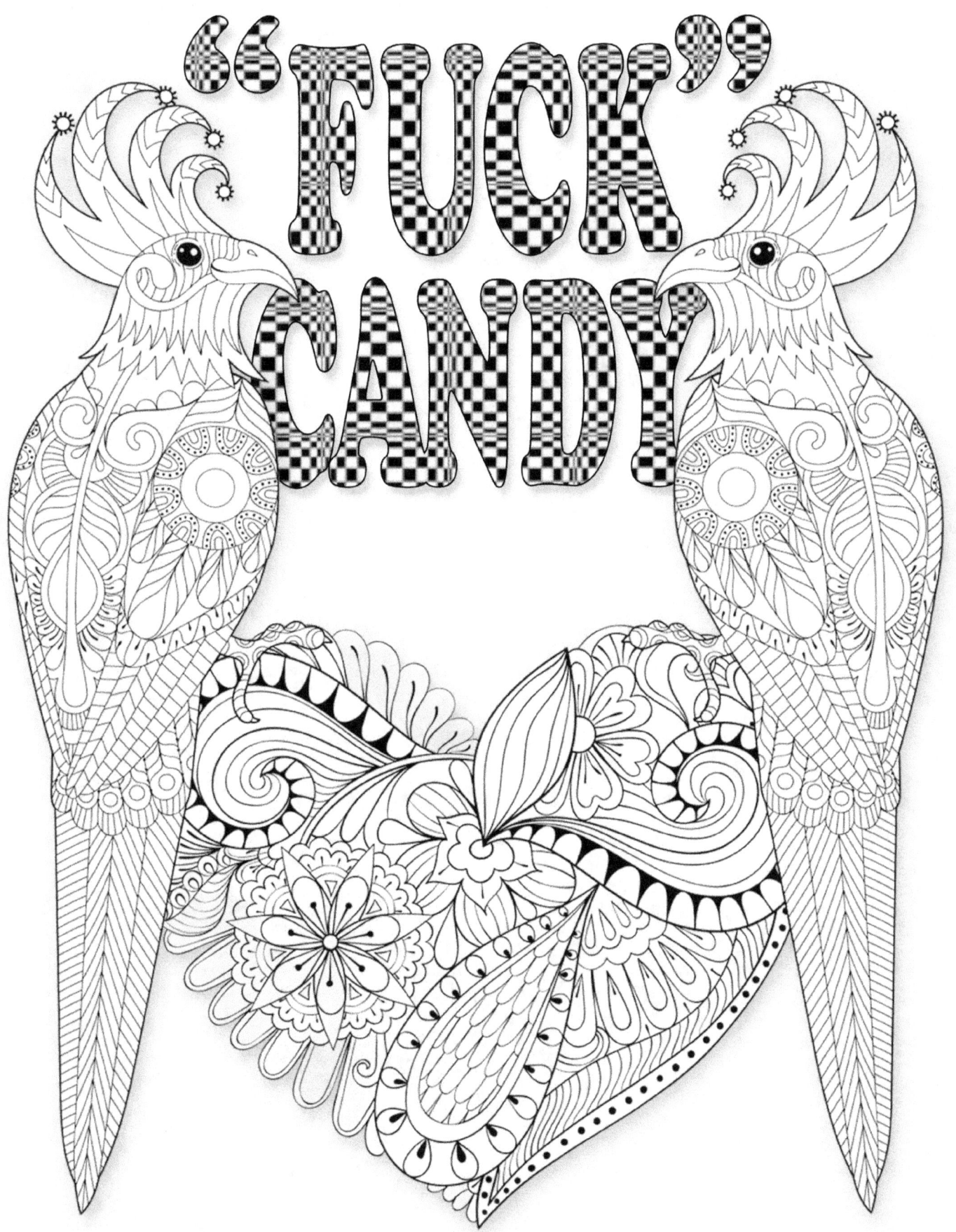

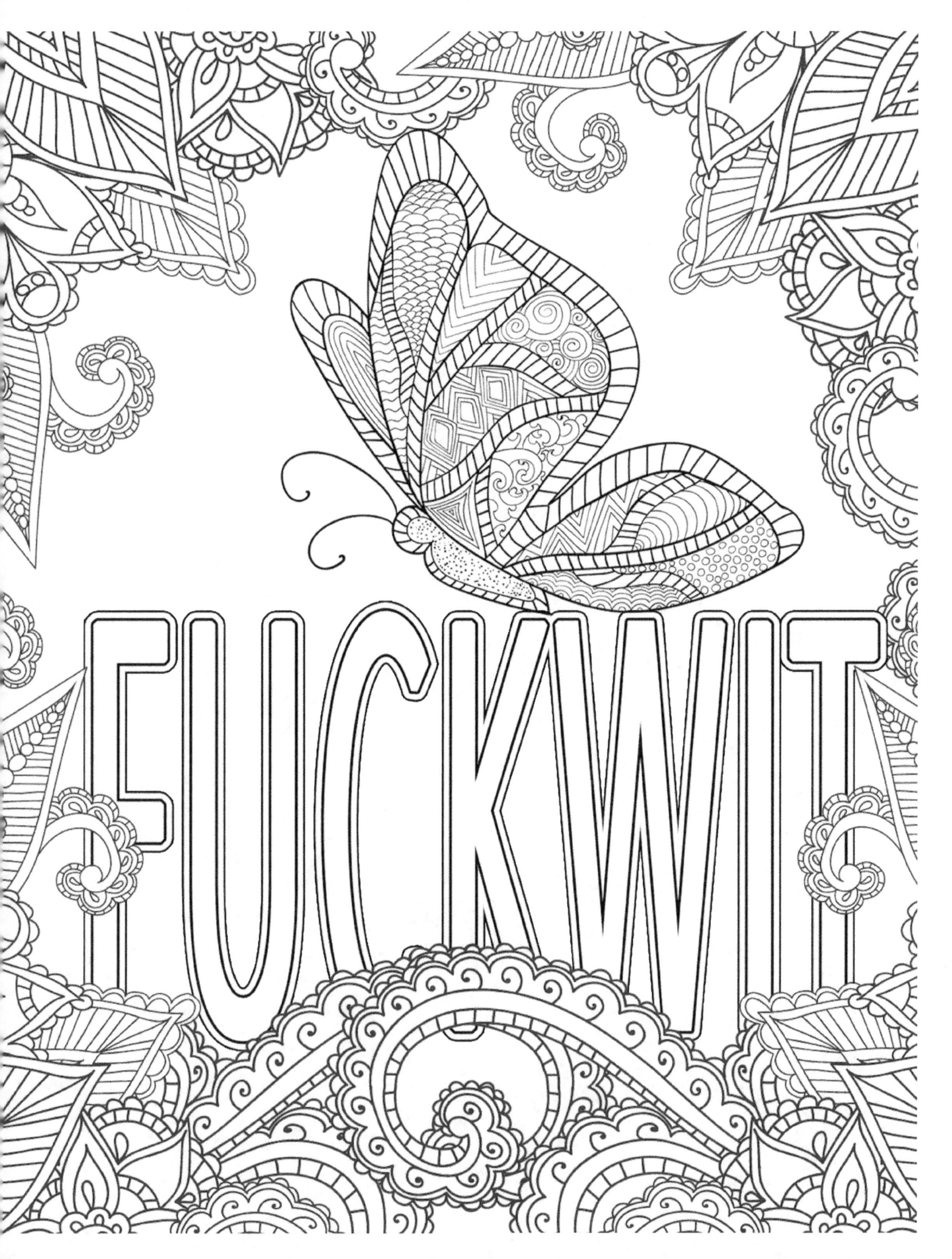

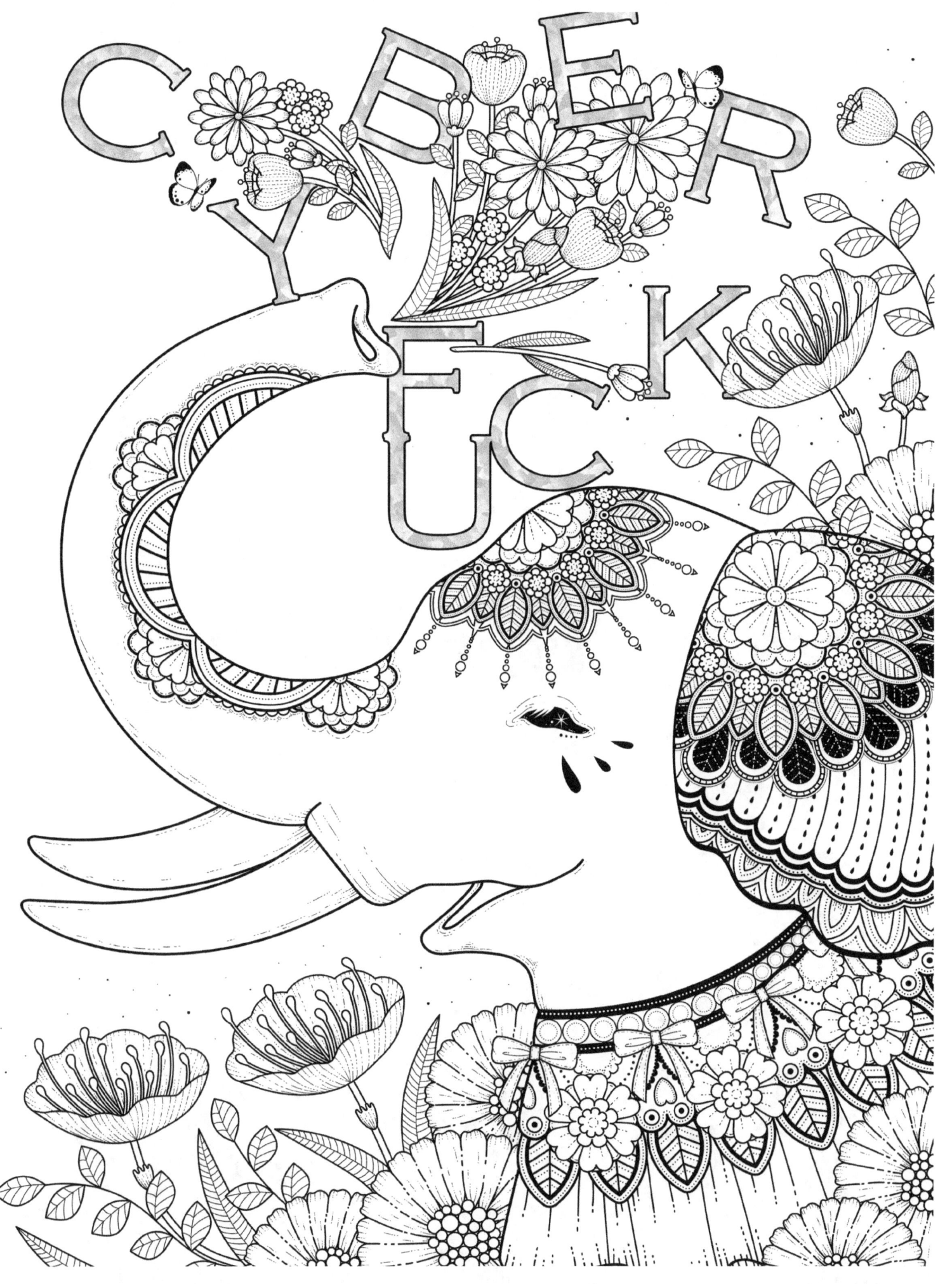

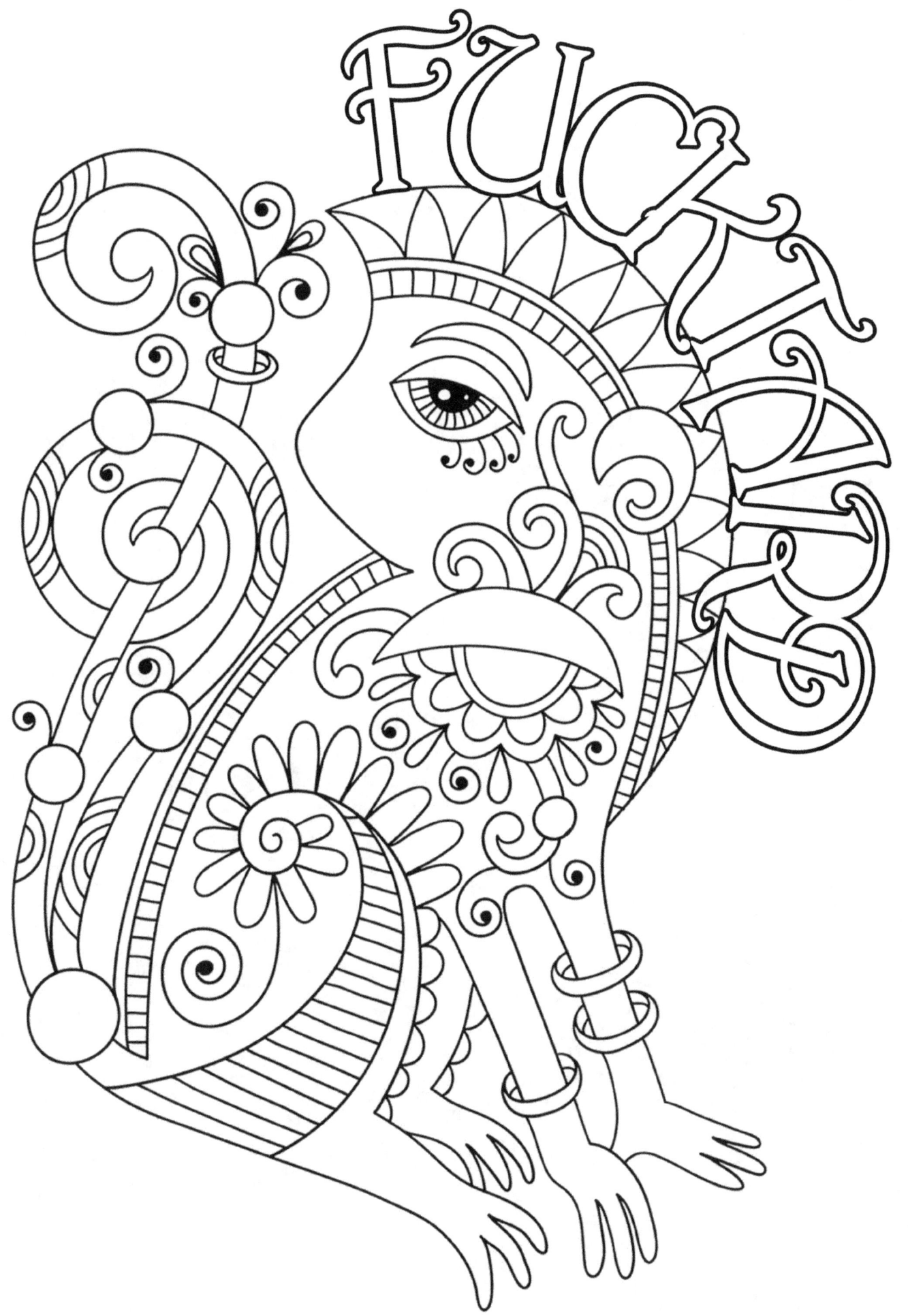

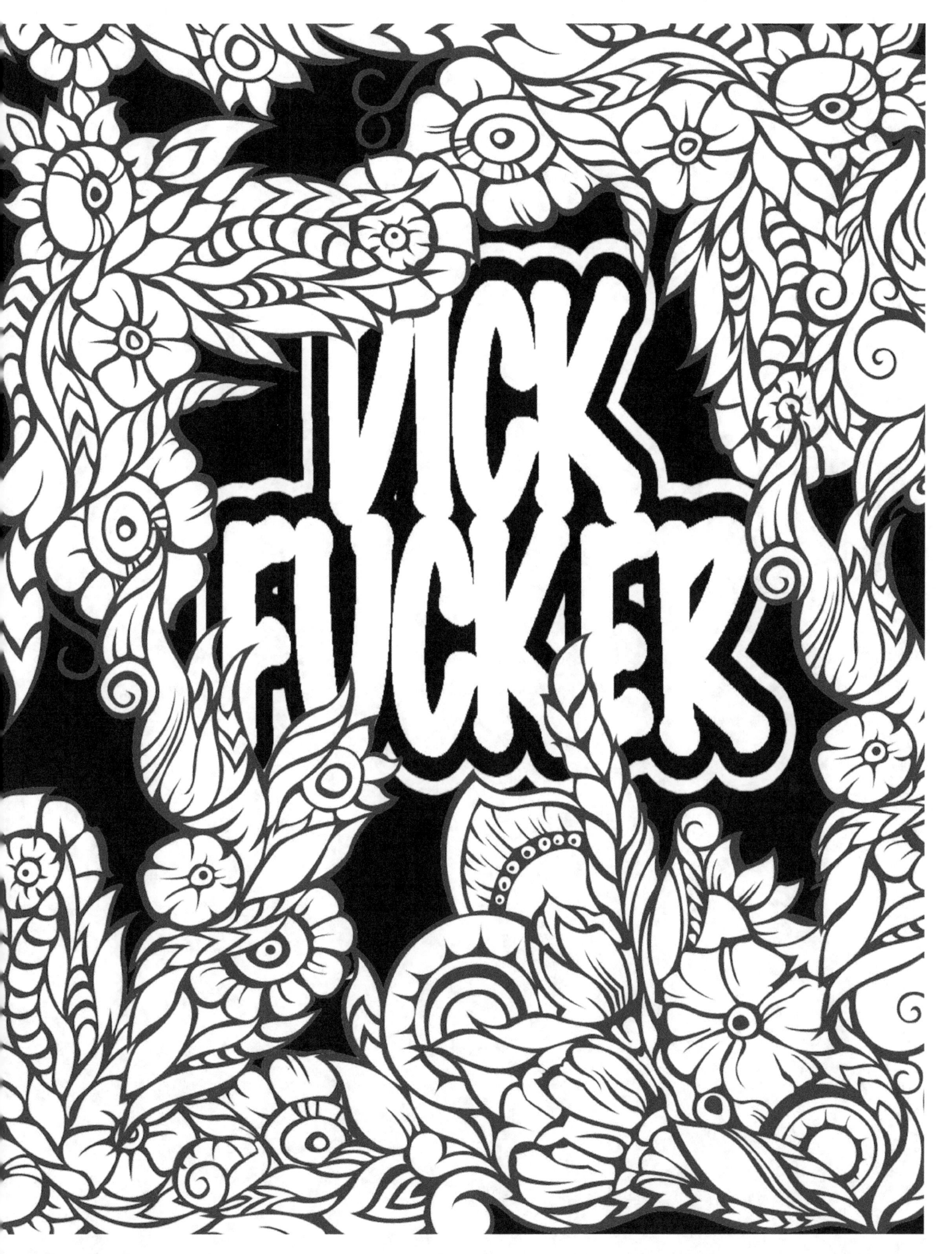

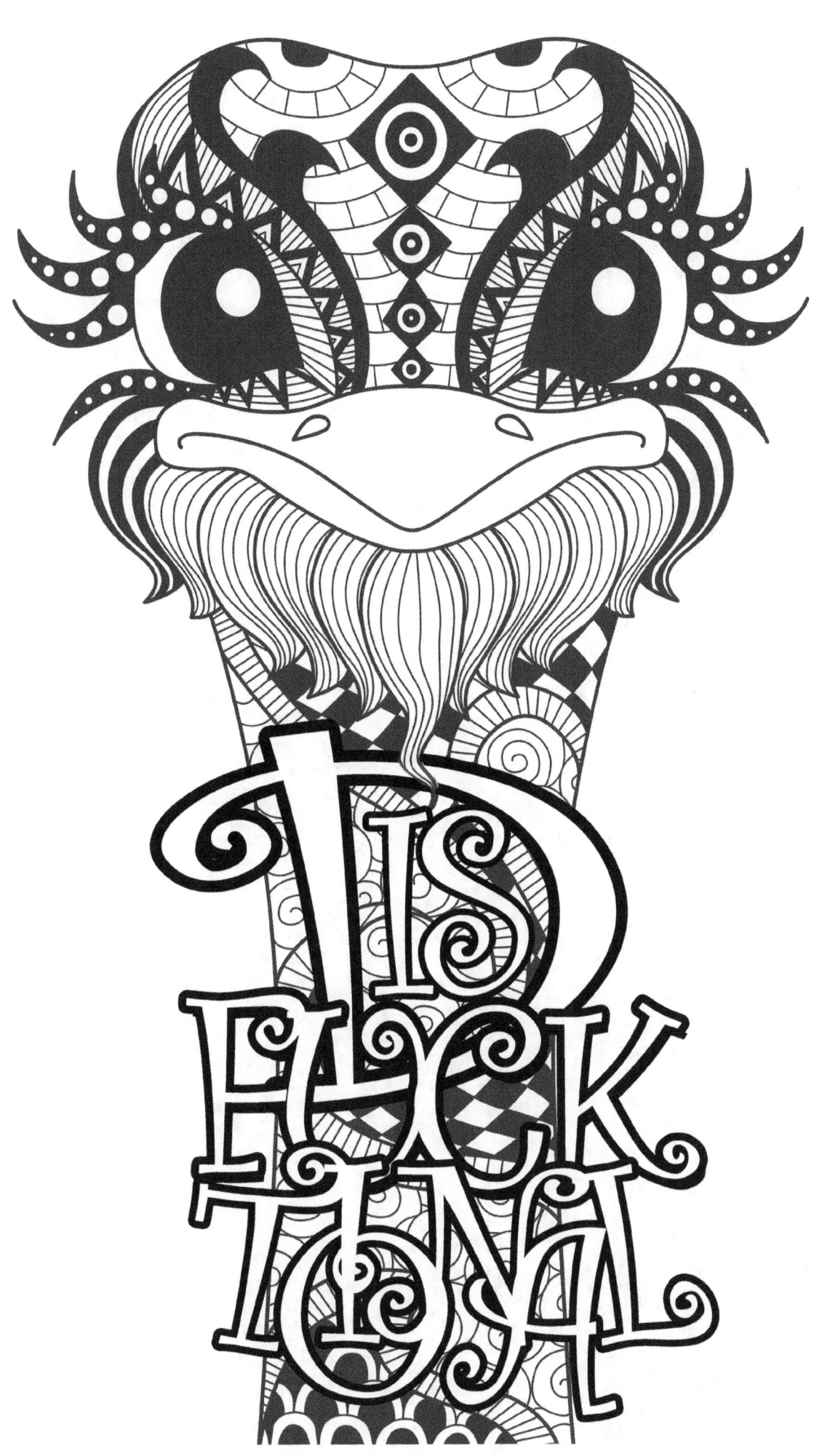

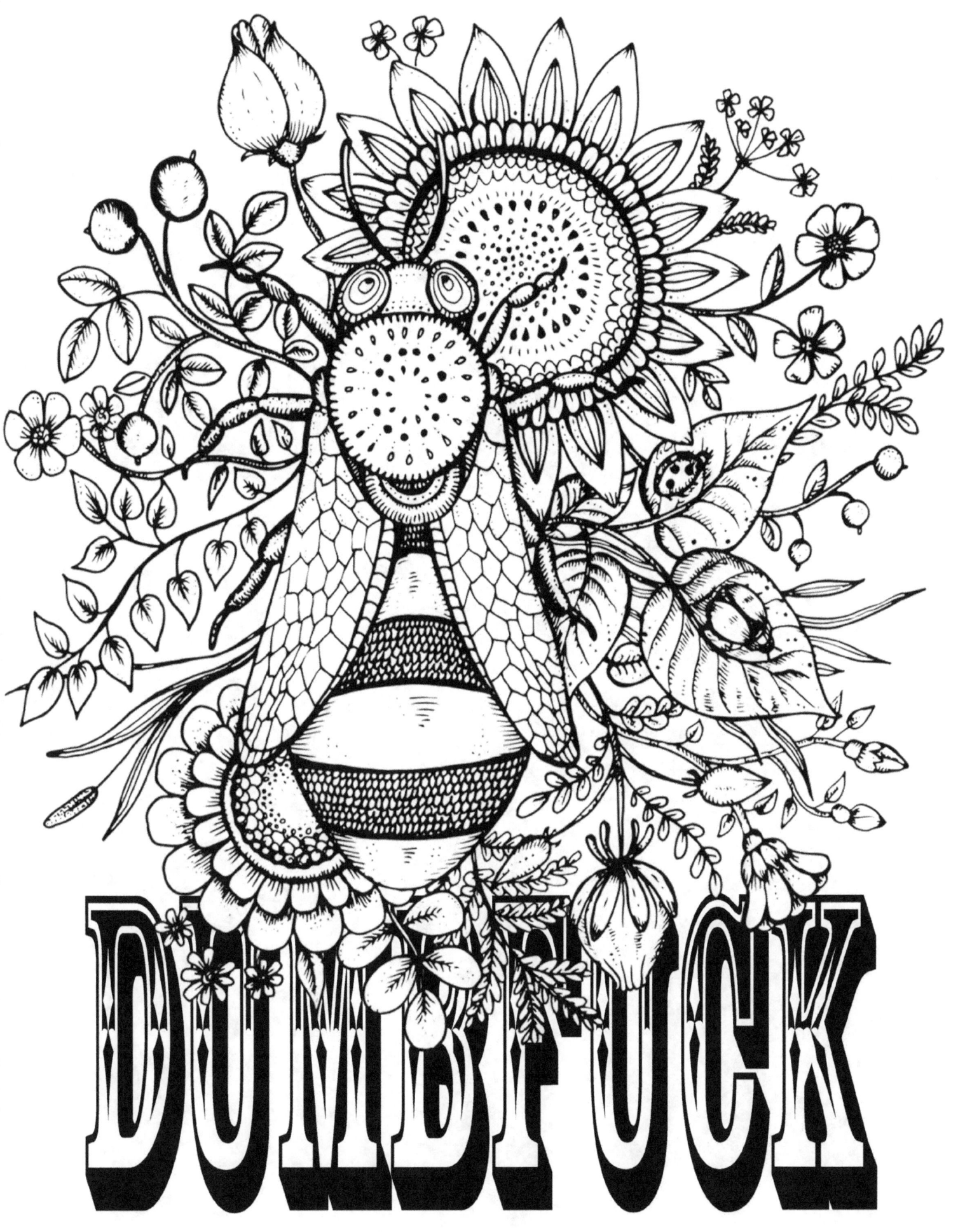

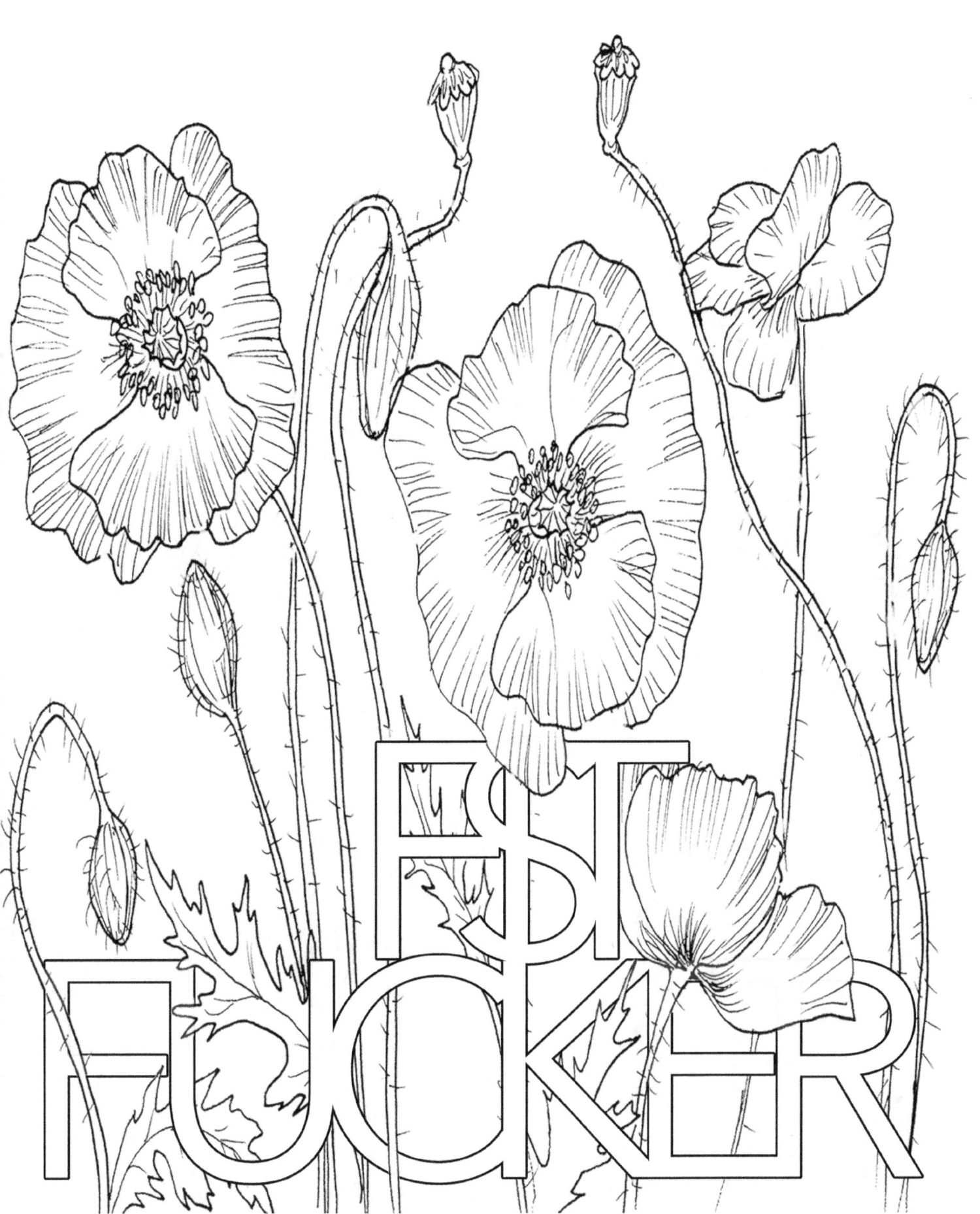

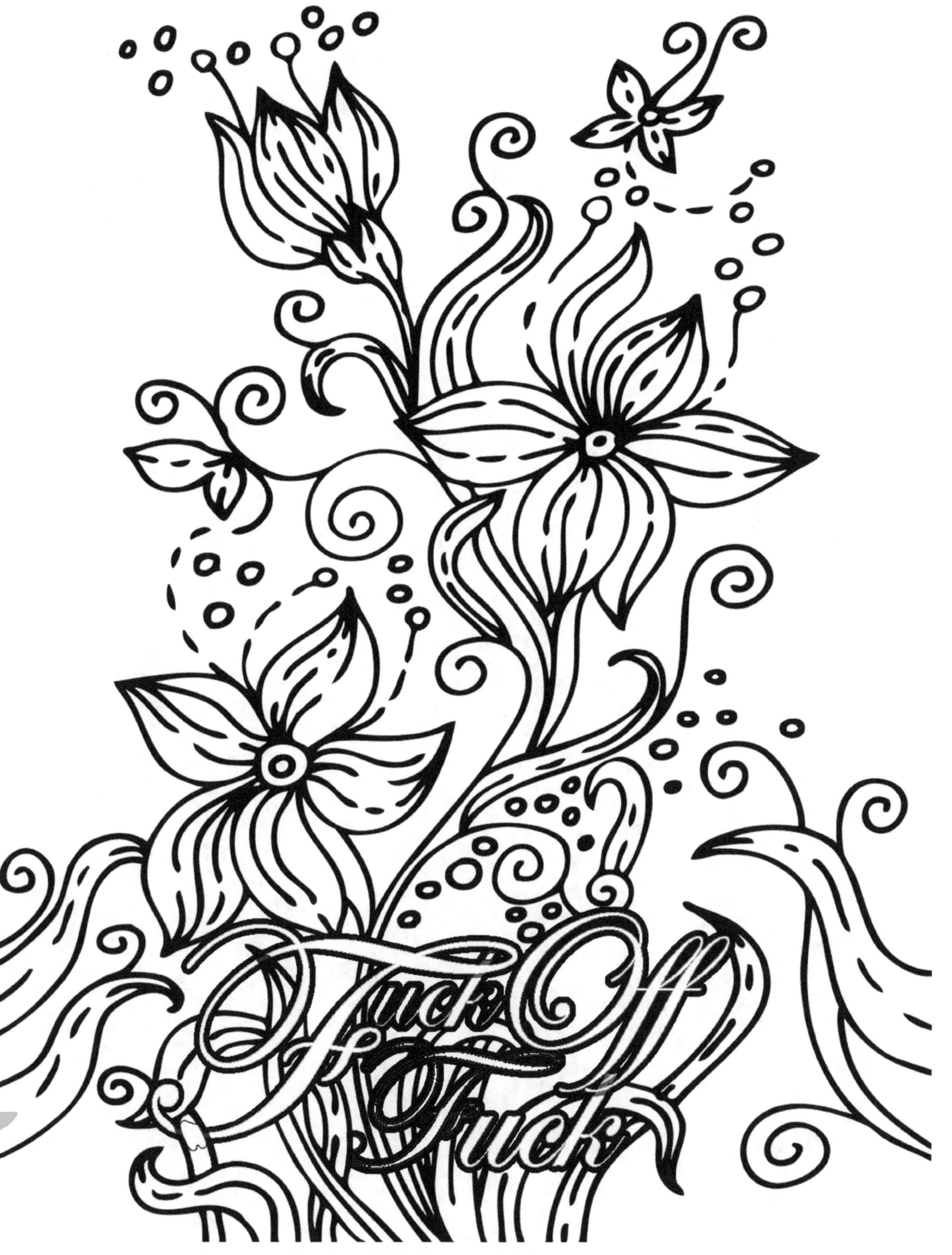

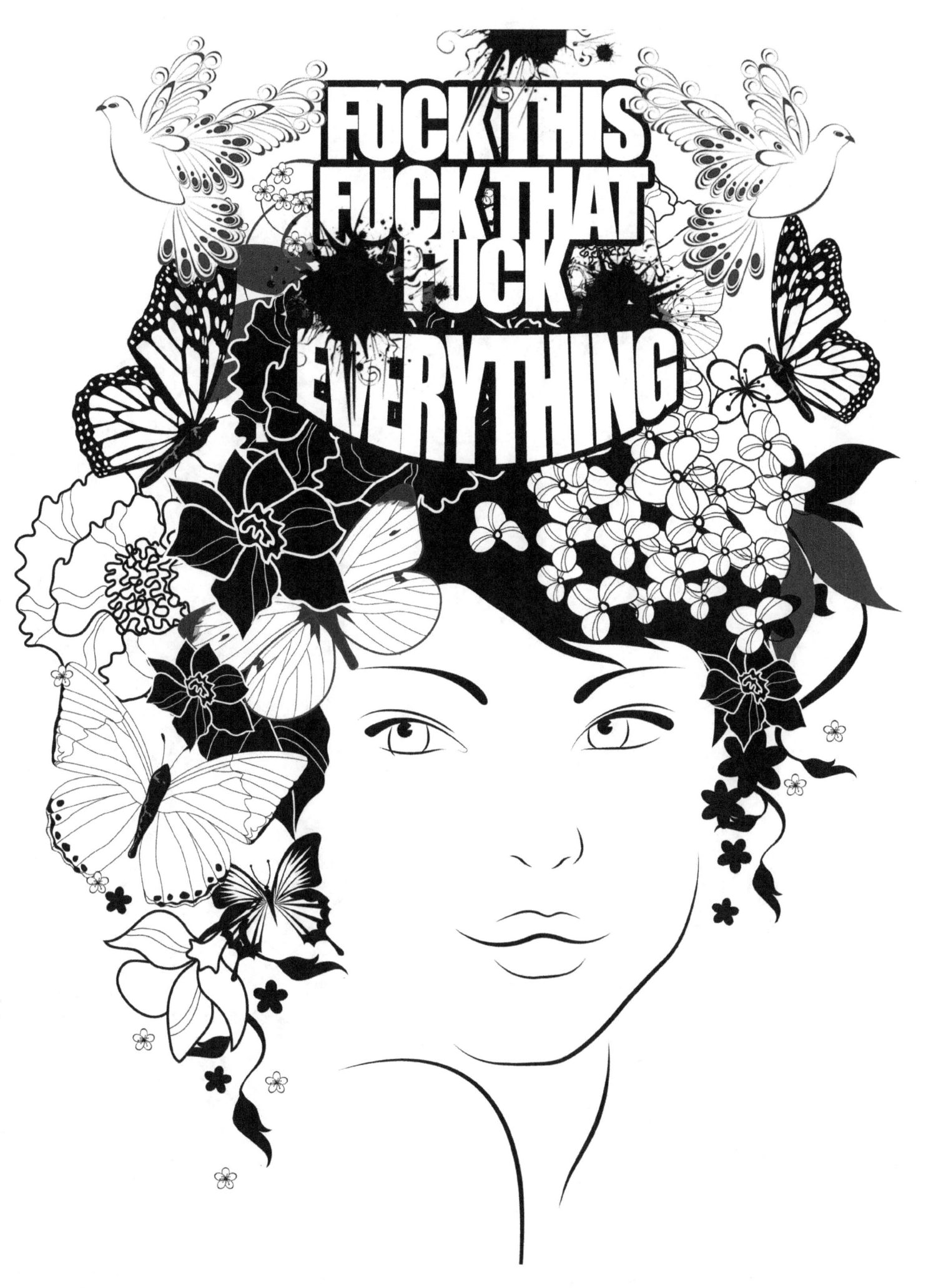

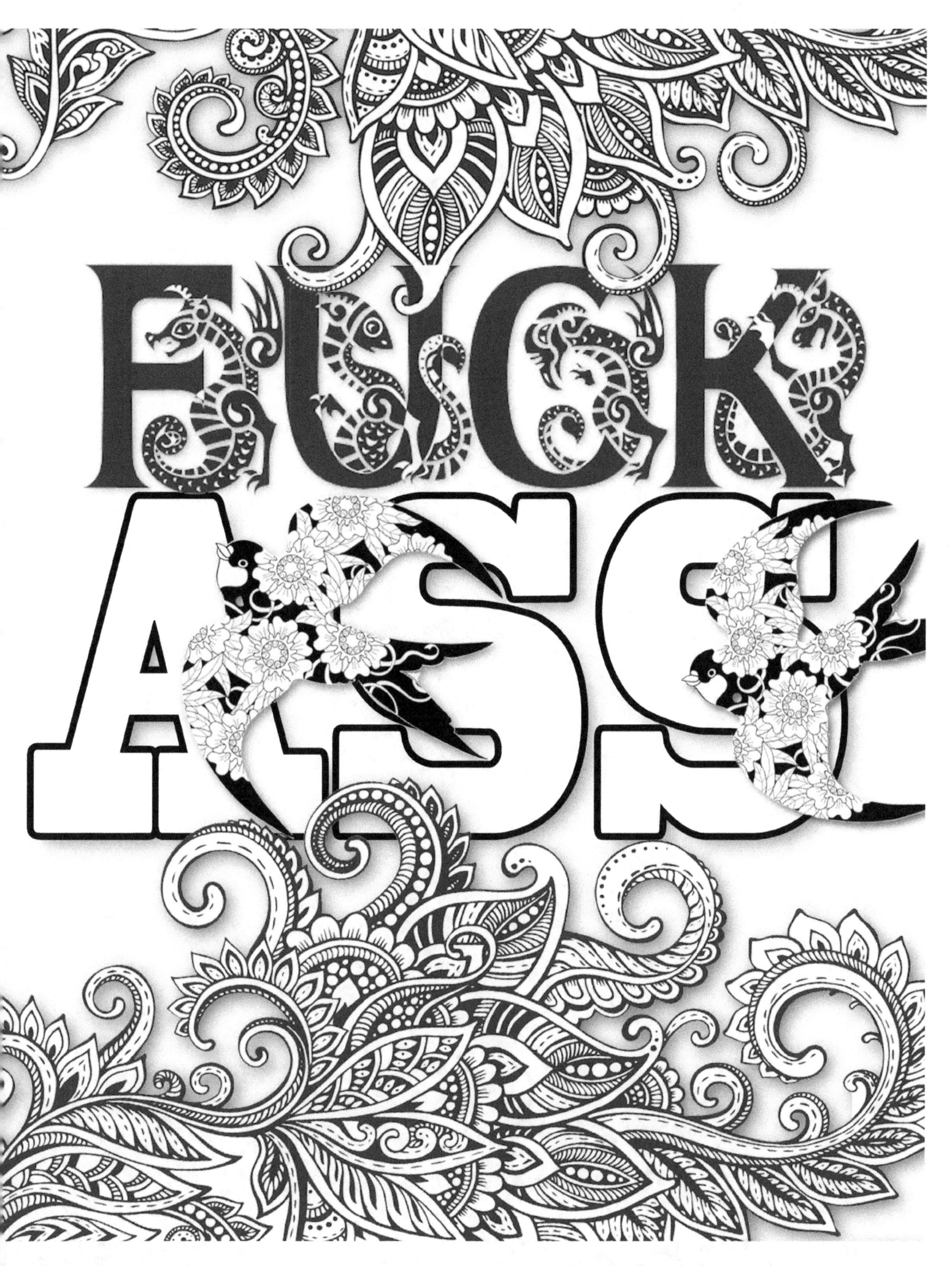

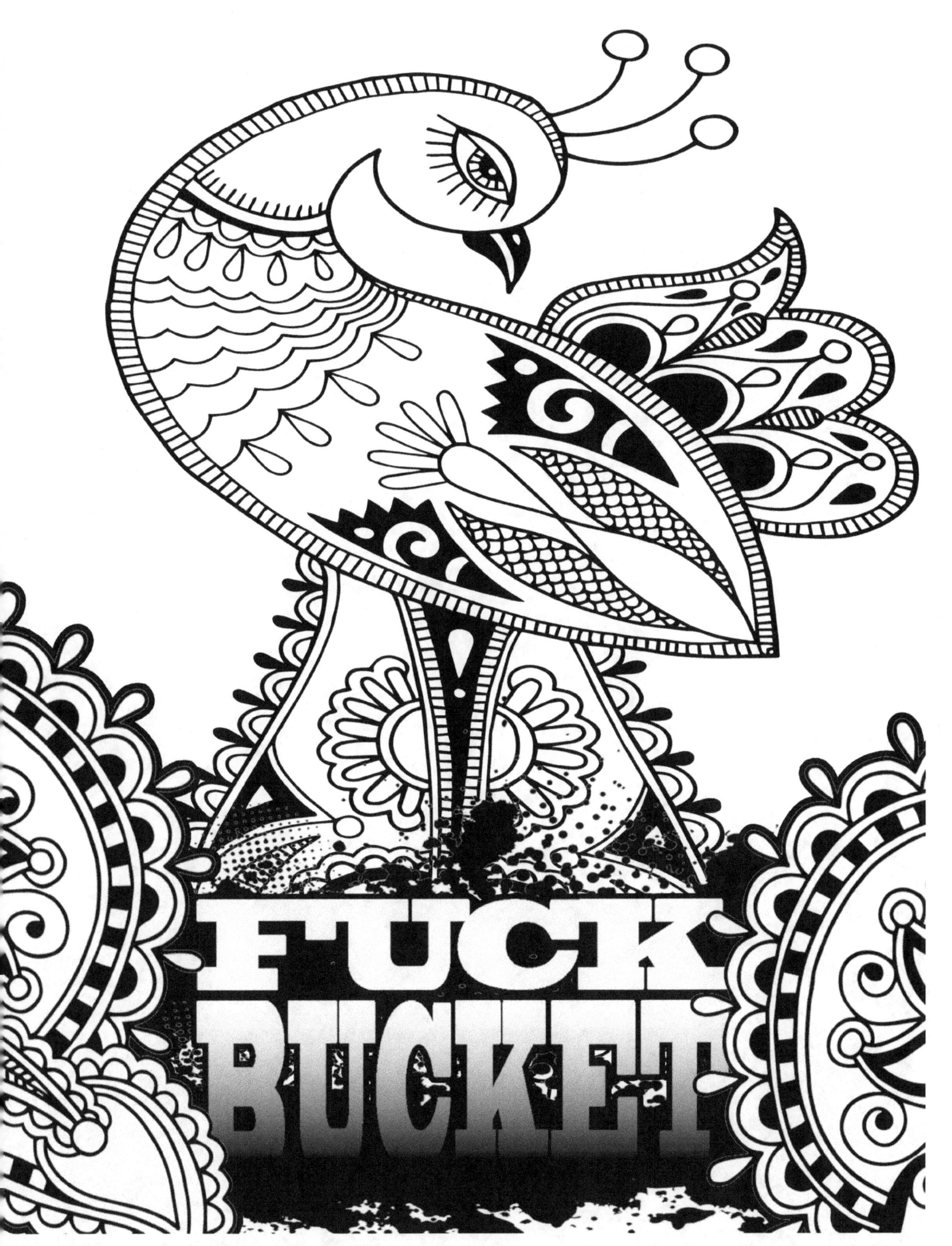

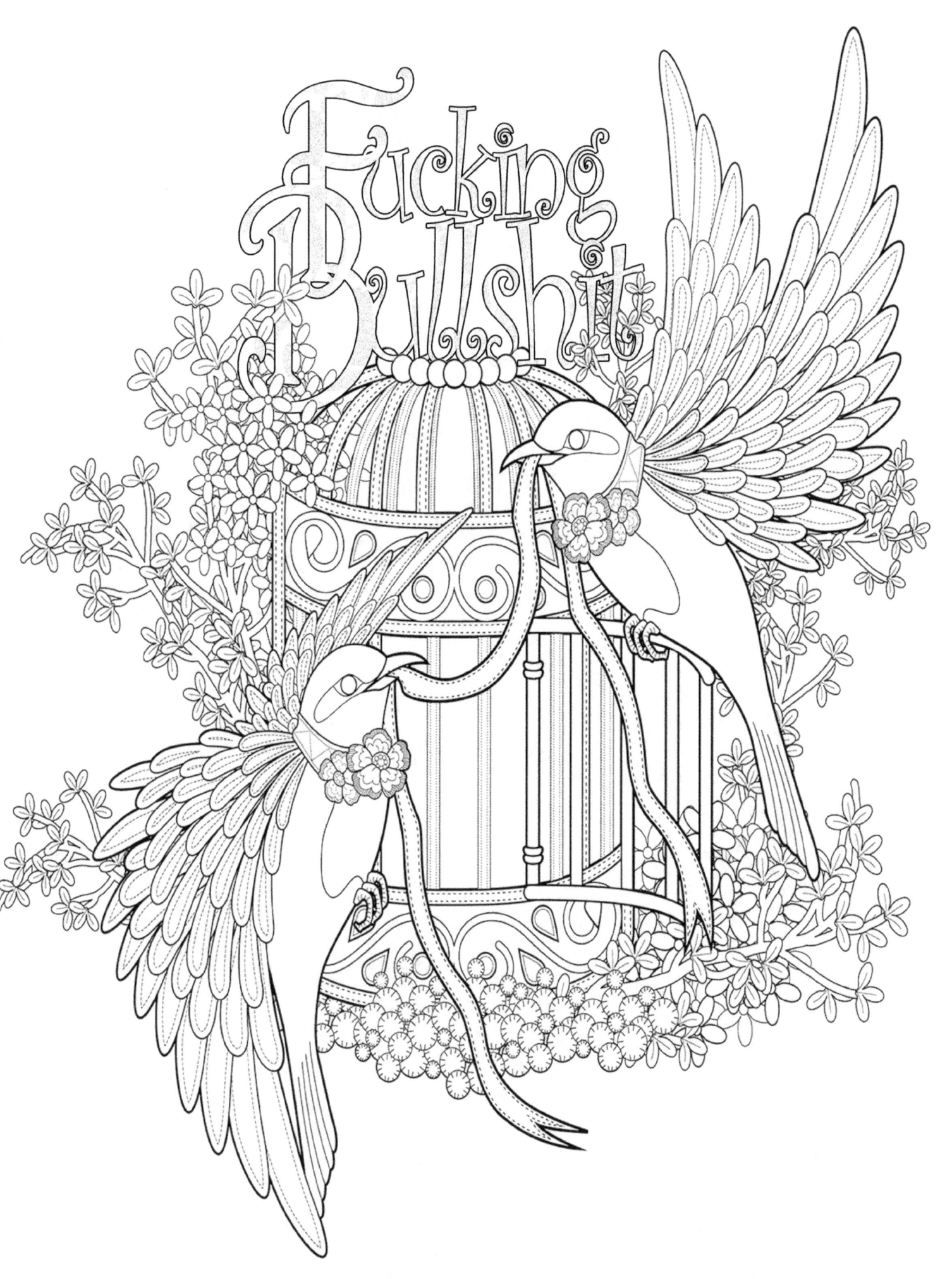

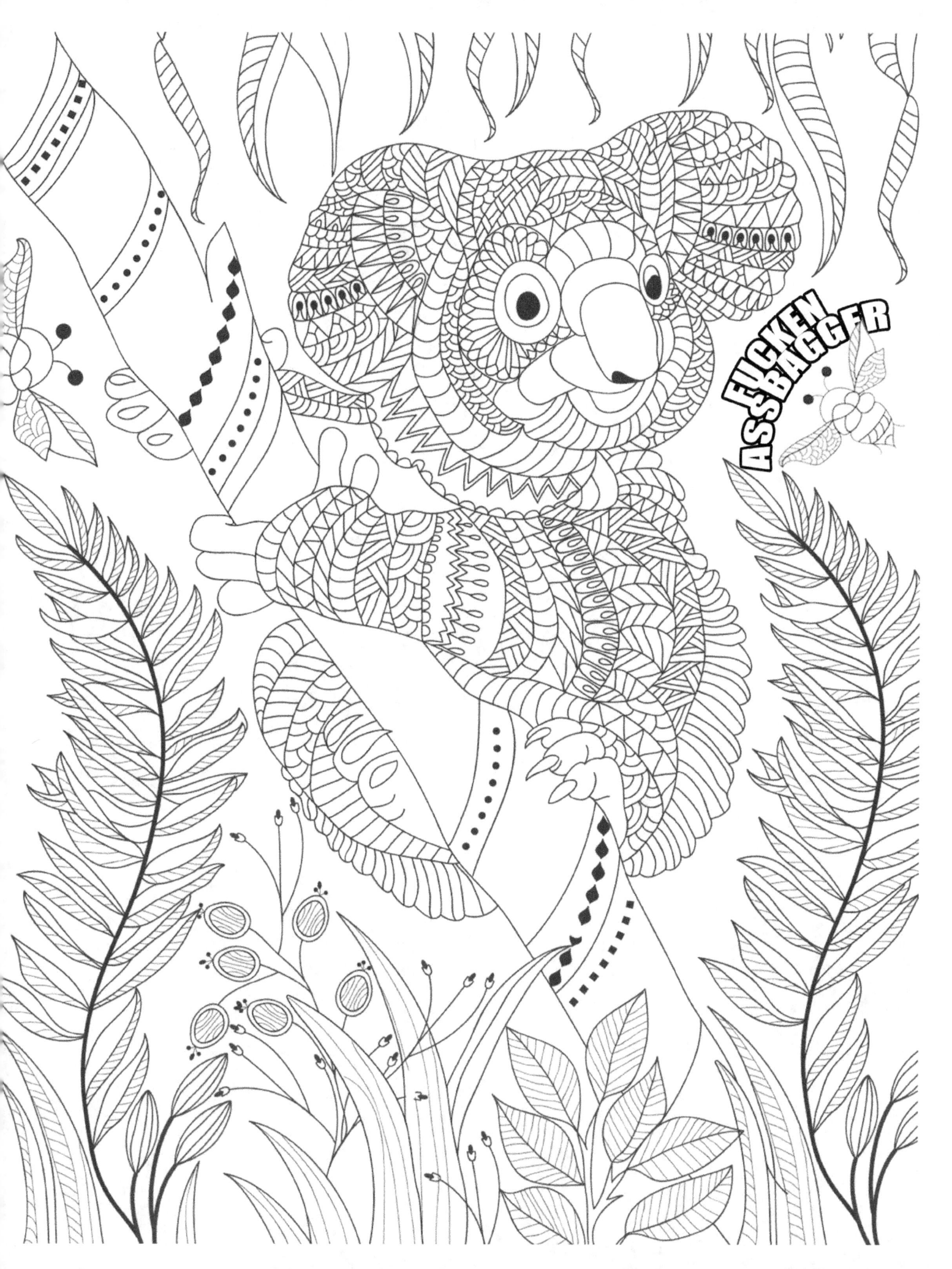

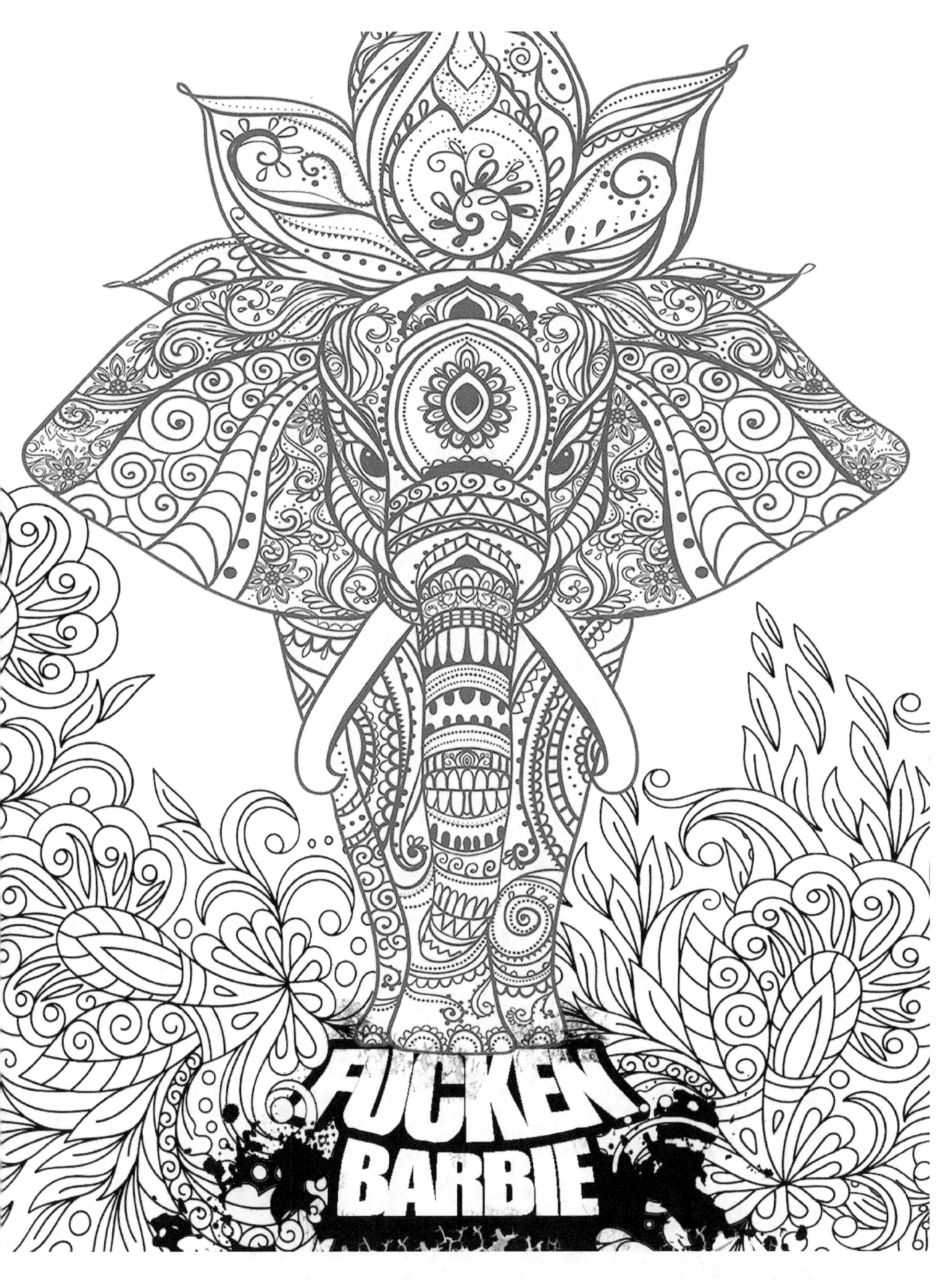

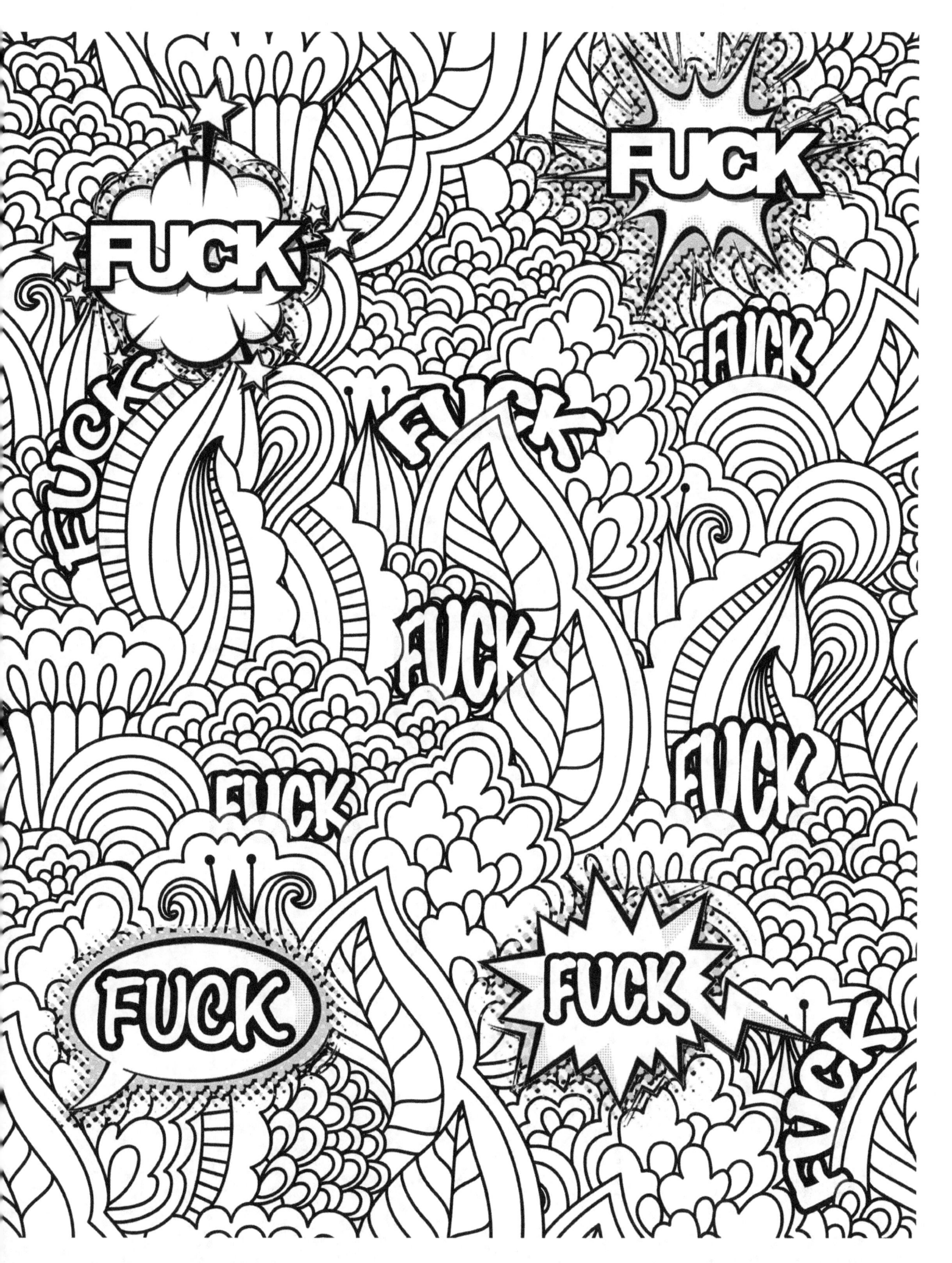

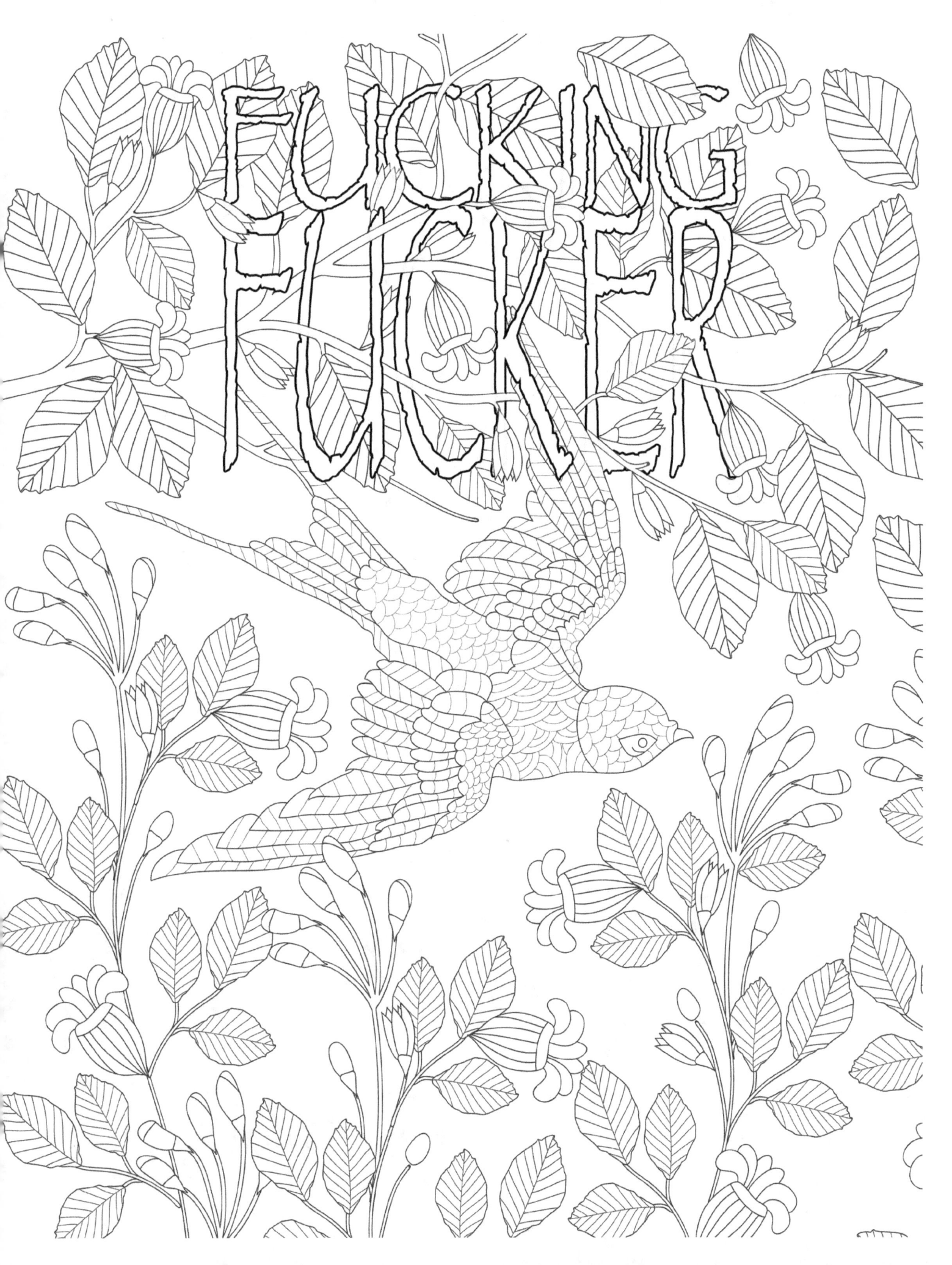

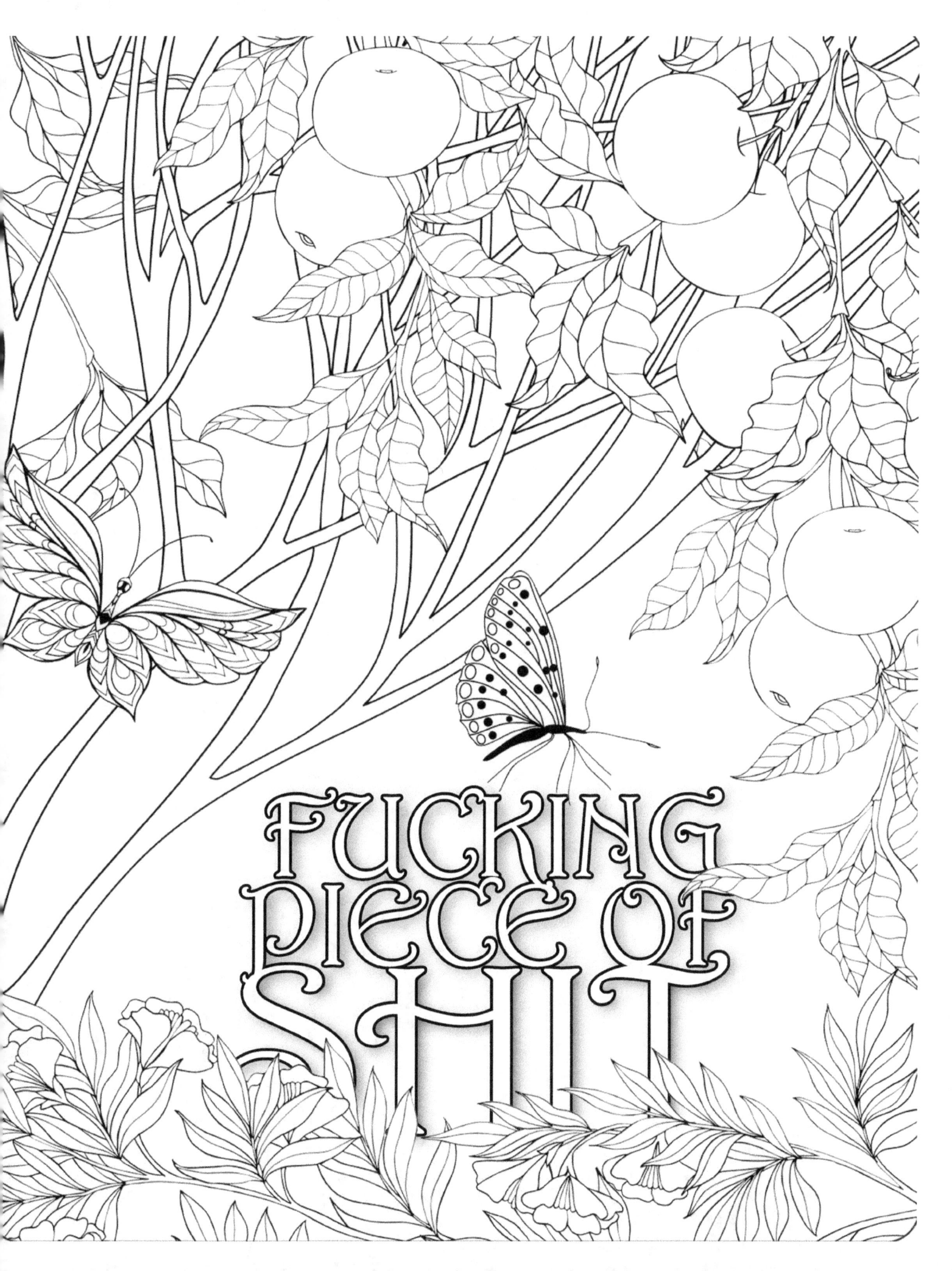

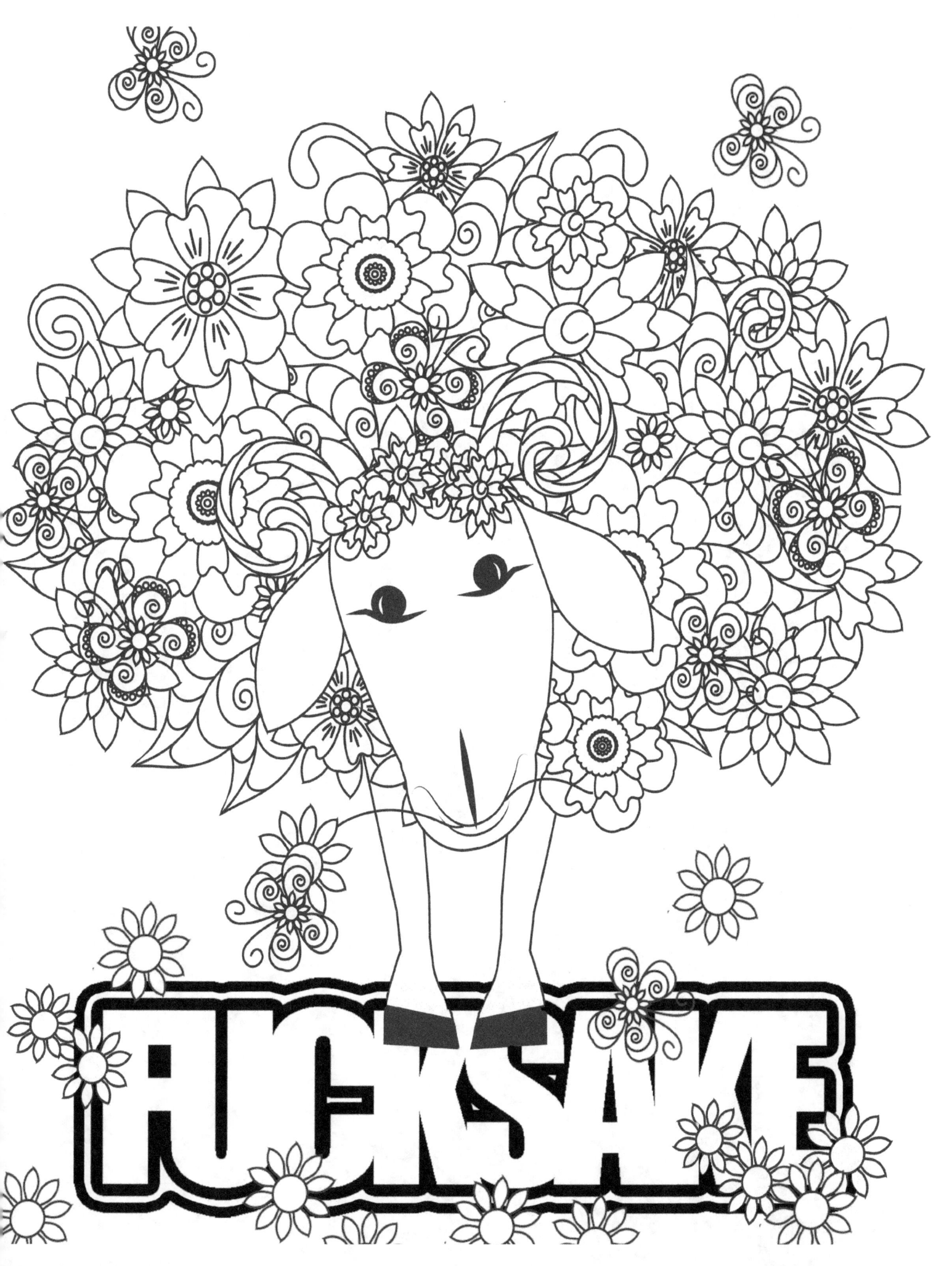

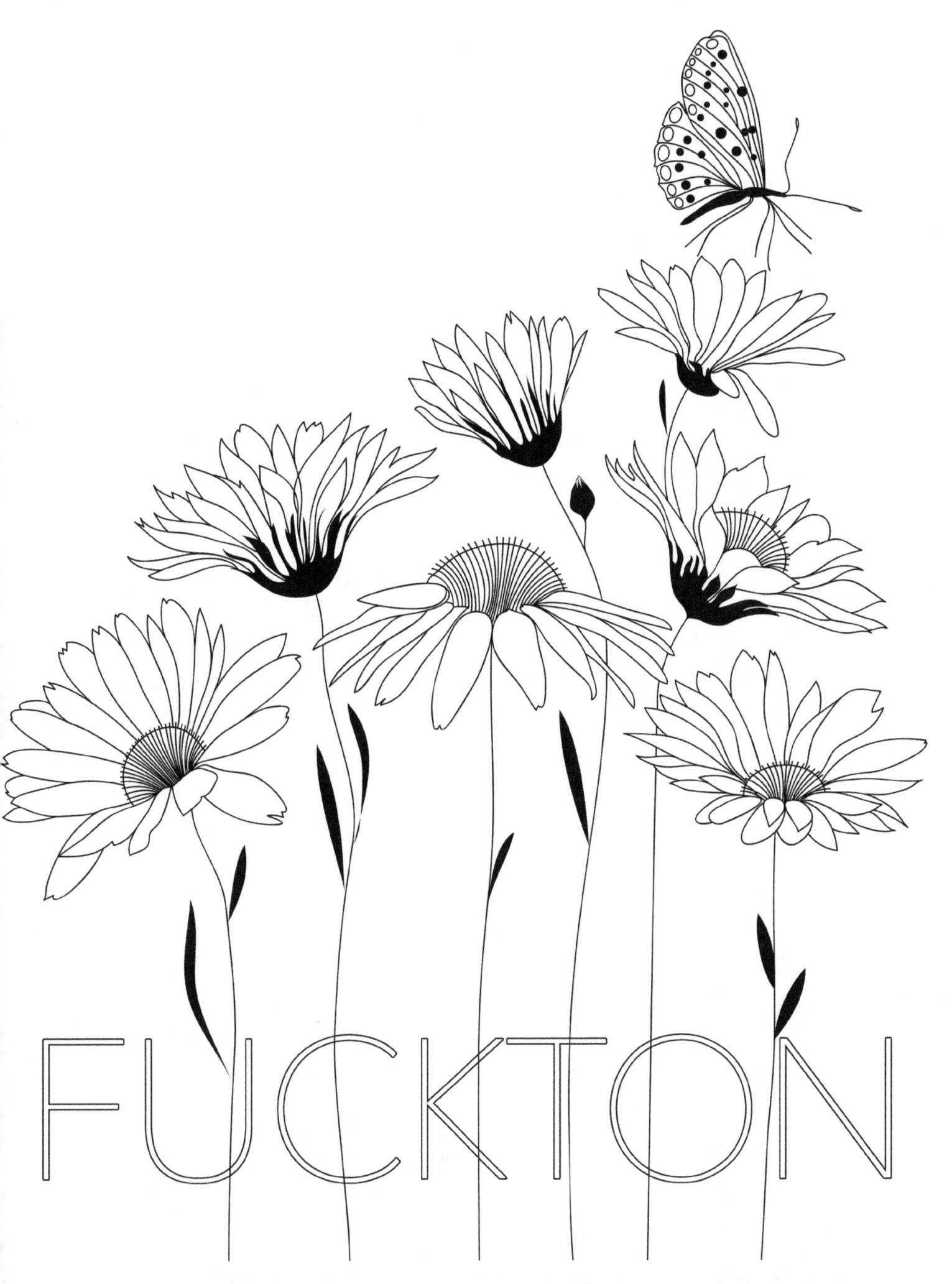

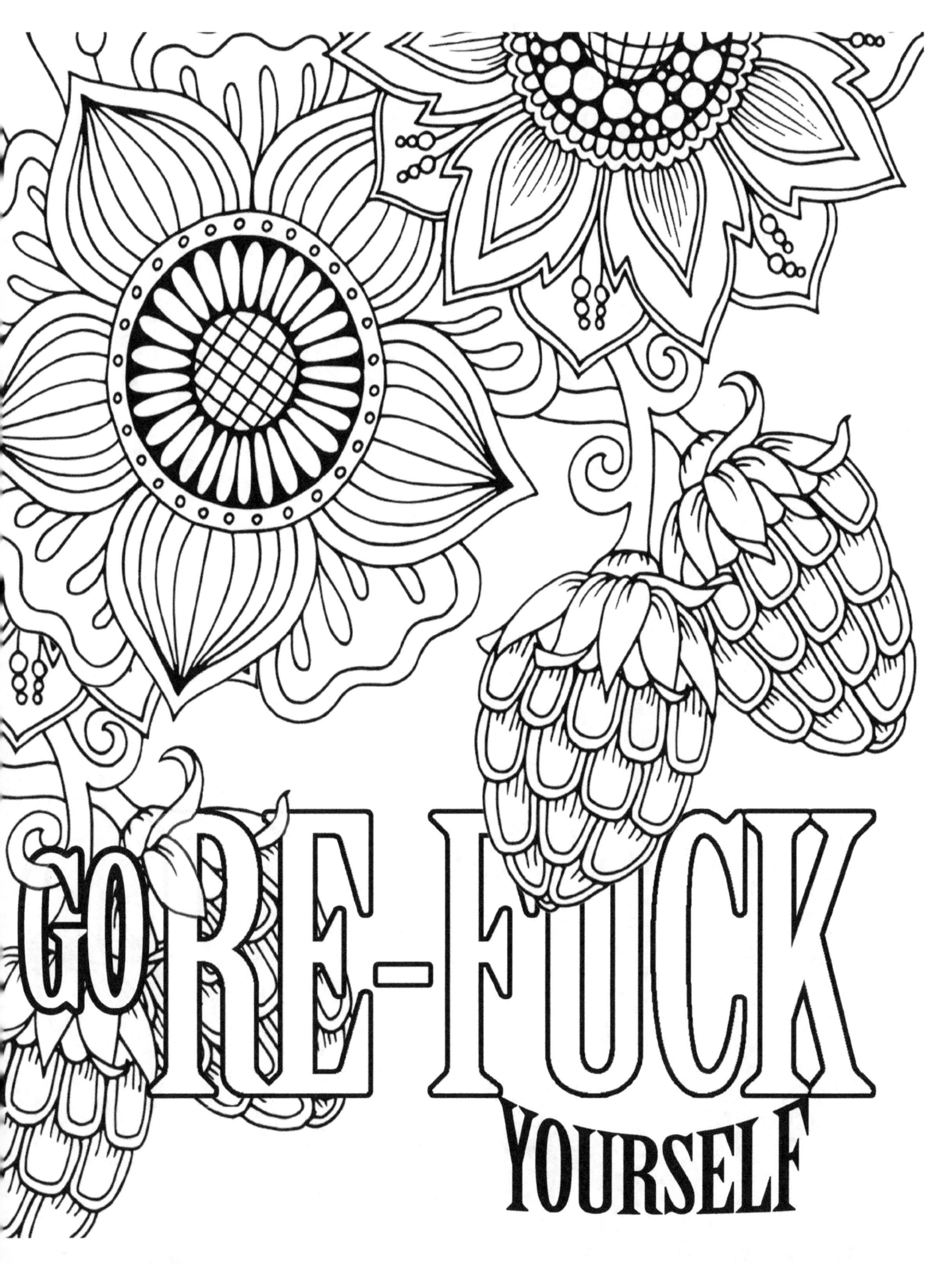

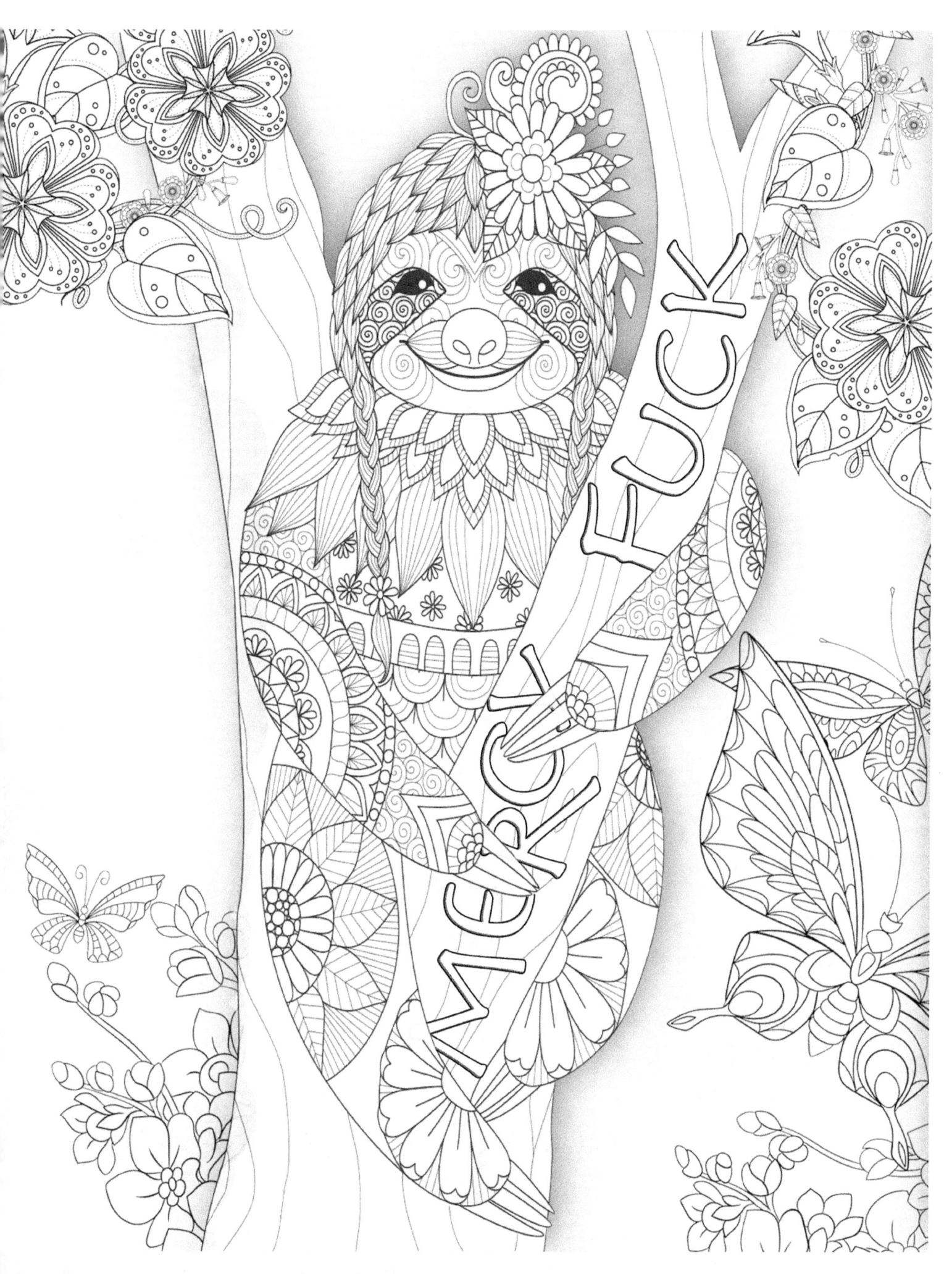

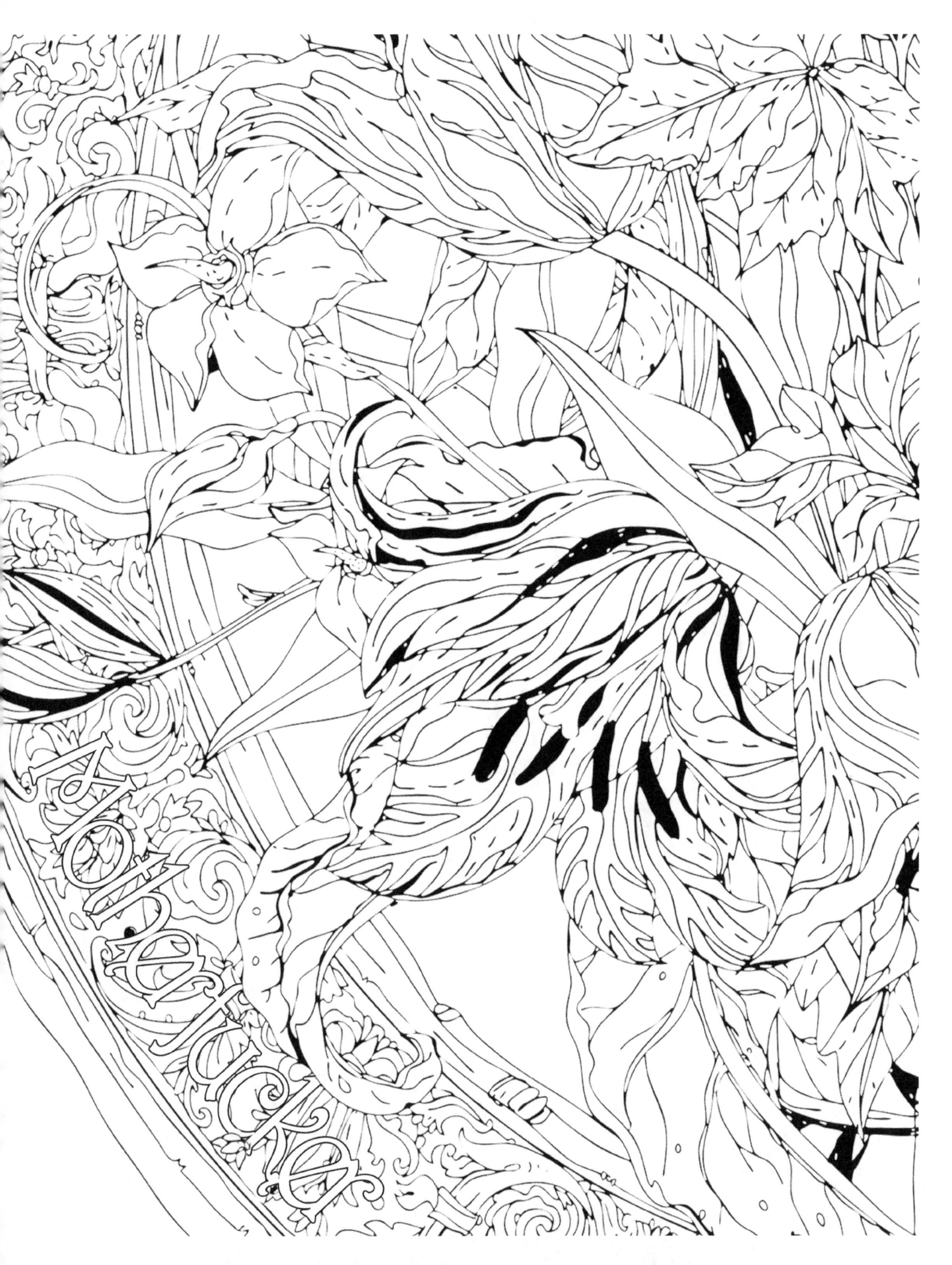

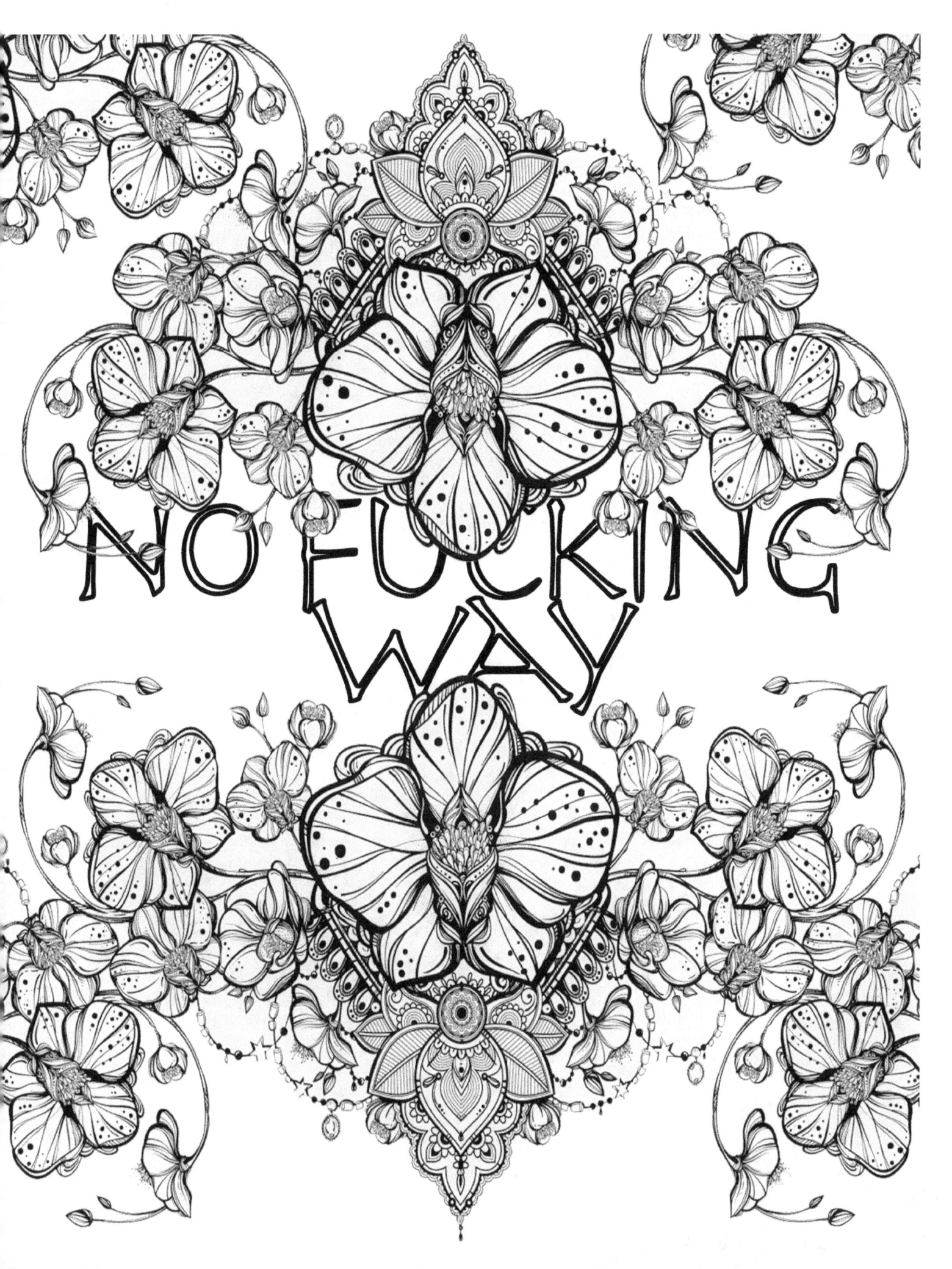

www.ingramcontent.com/pod-product-compliance
Lightning Source LLC
Chambersburg PA
CBHW080847170526
45158CB00009B/2658